TOUCHÉ

IN MEMORY OF MY THEORIES VOL. 2

WAVE BOOKS   SEATTLE AND NEW YORK

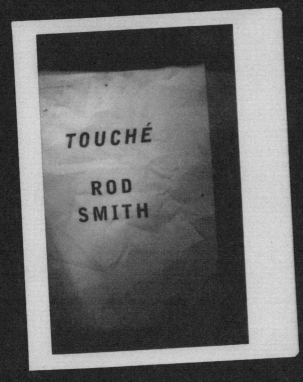

TOUCHÉ

ROD
SMITH

PUBLISHED BY WAVE BOOKS

WWW.WAVEPOETRY.COM

WAVE BOOKS TITLES ARE DISTRIBUTED TO THE TRADE BY

CONSORTIUM BOOK SALES AND DISTRIBUTION

PHONE: 800-283-3572 / SAN 631-760X

LIBRARY OF CONGRESS CATALOGING-IN-PUBLICATION DATA

SMITH, ROD, 1962–

[POEMS. SELECTIONS]

TOUCHÉ / ROD SMITH. — FIRST EDITION.

PAGES ; CM. — (IN MEMORY OF MY THEORIES ; VOL. 2)

ISBN 978-1-940696-07-2 (LIMITED EDITION HARDCOVER) —

ISBN 978-1-940696-08-9 (SOFTCOVER)

I. TITLE.

PS3569.M537962A6 2015

811'.54—DC23

2014026647

DESIGNED AND COMPOSED BY QUEMADURA

PRINTED IN THE UNITED STATES OF AMERICA

9 8 7 6 5 4 3 2 1

FIRST EDITION

WAVE BOOKS 049

for Mel

TOUCHÉ

The Birds of America

The tall
beach
&
the same
classic
certainty.

Thirty-four
expert
mirroring
impediments, casual
& dusty grey,
peering—a fourth
of the fifth
cordless
ginmill
cut open
keeps awake
the
honed
windows &
grates.

The Story of Mang Gong

after I flew off the top of the car
into a bag
that broke I said "shit"
& I just lie there a long time &
nothing else ever happened again.
the end.

& then I didn't get enough sleep & I feel like
Spit
The world has lots of strips
Otter
As kind individual keeping
If you ask me a question
I will hit you thirty times
Then,
I won't ask you a question—
The rum tastes late
The hurricane is kept in the petri dish &
There is no light rain
Time to leave the ending on the miniature war's nascent
butt buying new software won't help
It's told to lean on it to keep it from copping some loaded
cut offs &
cleans it up to say to you

& you & you
this type of thing
& jade &
the raided localities keep linking
summer to a certain kind of heat &
the worst thing about getting older is realizing
the lie inherent in every emotional state so

I'll see you on or from the roof of
if I don't fall
on the other hand we are the unlikely beings
& our secret
is not to

talk about any one thing

Poem

                italic &
                crayolaed

lumps of
cordoned
mascaras
boil
  your
heartfelt
massacres,
puppyhead—
        depth
        of cloak &
        repercipient
        neighbobs
        bump-up
        wisdom's
nurturing colonialisme—

the representation *of the working class has become*
the enemy *of the working class—*

read the nightlike bias into *the barrister—*

Gumby likes your tabac . . . *his toothlike winsome wants*
are territory   are the ancient stain we fell   & rein

I am no I I slight

I've taught myself to unwrite
& then wreathed, saturate, blank
the severed glinting worlds rebelieve
or they all access overall not-so, a not-so
lucid, a lucid one, the squirrels that I live there
^.^ ~ alright then, alright mr squirrel there, yep.

Police Poem

Grace to be killed and die as brainlessly as political
The fiefed beasts &

\\ 'hons' unarrested in the trail pack tax . . .

*the proletariat's determining role in history stopped
with the bombing of Hiroshima*

unbest

bright

chide

light-aright of an ink-fest army-civ this weed arose from the civilian code(s)
a complex assonance the sages succeed in, weed-tested and in that brood a jolly cap-
tain's *new freedom* it has four heads and gulps computer juice like power organized
by one class to suppress another but i know as we all know Miket and a sergeant
named Healey . . .

cops just arrest people

capitularies & helots
accentuate the sacred power of yoga.

base tame mild-mannered look-away american methologies of enchambered meri-ken class-struggle—its archetype is the cursory execution of every ninth one in line—a 64th of the needed semi-wild flock (People all know the workings of order and chaos) People all know the map they showed us. People all know the gravity of advancement within the strong force. Their vital spirits are guarded within

and cannot be deluded by things. Things, however, are quite deluded.

IN A STATION OF THE METRO

The apparition of these faces in the crowd;

Passed out beside the litterbox.

dumb poem

Andy Warhol tries lols kittehs
This is a big deal because it's the first time
Andy Warhol. "What's the deal?"
I have Warhol coasters, and love his brown
Rambo and his green cokes
hit my line i got
what's your favorite movie home decor?
hit my line i got
Your Nose Record your own or Listen
what's the deal I mean,
several poems deal with Warhol's near-death after the 1968
Q&A
"But there's a great deal of substance here." IF YOU GO.
WHAT?
what a foolish man
yo yoyo yo i dig the diy dinosaur lamps
it creates great deal
line of sneakers
hit my line i got
what's your favorite movie home decor?
That's what Warhol's religion really comes down to.
Warhol's Portrait of Michael Jackson Temporarily Pulled from Auction
in the Hamptons. . . . . . And you are asking what? what.
does this have to do with me?

hit my line i got

what's your favorite movie home decor?

heterosexual, motorcycle-riding, breakfast modifying line of sneakers

hit my line i got

line of sneakers

hit my line i got

line of sneakers

what's your favorite heterosexual?

what's your favorite dinosaur lamp?

1.0 out of 5 stars Minor dealer finds minor Warhol - big deal.

line of sneakers

deal wit the negativities in life that define

What is that horrendous monstrosity?

based on your photo.

line of sneakers

based on your photo.

He gets Warhol on the phone. I mean you could do that in those days, . . .

line of sneakers

based on your photo.

line of sneakers

Ellis Takes the Plea Deal

line of sneakers

based on your photo.

line of sneakers

And unemployment

omgbobzerillia added What's Your Poo Telling. . . . . .

based on your photo.

And unemployment

omgbobzerillia added What's Your Poo Telling. . . . . .

based on your photo.

omgbobzerillia added What's Your Poo Telling. . . . . .

That's what is really insulting not Warhol.

hit my line i got

line of sneakers

hit my line i got

And unemployment

The French still saw Warhol in epic terms. 'He reigns over a sunless

line of sneakers

based on your photo

What's the deal????

unemployment

According to Wrbican, Warhol did not . . . uh, ok, isn't it?

which was largely made before they got a

China

snowboard

What's the point of a smoking mouth?

deal wit the negativities in life that define

Teddy King (King

Teddy King (King

Teddy King (King

hit my line i got

Teddy King (King

Teddy King (King

Teddy King (KingTeddy King (King

Teddy King (King

line of sneakers

Teddy King (King

hit my line i got

Teddy King (KingTeddy King (King

Teddy King (KingTeddy King (KingTeddy King (KingTeddy King (KingTeddy

King (King
Teddy King (King
hit my line i got
hit my line i got
hit my line i got
Teddy King (King
Teddy King (KingTeddy King hit my line i got Teddy Teddy (King King

andy warhol, what
what

Needed a Kite &

Spoke stupid

Some stalled combination
of onions   & lotion   & onions,   their
        opined options jet-blue involved Off &
        glucose chiming happenstances hoo-do-dooed on
a hazard floor—
I'm kinda glowing & pucks are onions

The loam has a nippy blood-nut to let us in on.

Oren Gates

The trusted, inchoate
bleeding canvas
bag
the planed
aspirin taker
talks to them
tells the family
the soldier they raised
should not be opened.

PoÔem

neither & not
have accessed
the everclear, ornately—it's got
crude (or diurnal) brick
biases pasted on its pudenda—

the mock
& the meaning interpenetrate in the peace,
running your life—

o Larry, how might, like a performative self-contradiction
our unauthorized tutorials bump the grime from the co-fed
impy mongrels of fate?

hmm.

PoÔem 2

cordless lord of copious nukes, deep
in the Ahab of some theory of the *destruckticon*

i love measel squall. i love the round right of romanticism.

leave the each alone, the letters
comfort in this the winding made to part.

la la la

Hmm. (PoÔem 3)

a certain deeply attentive slouch will bring down the upper class

me, mostly pocket home floods, mostly climb the plagiarism mushroom.

if the surgery takes, shouldn't we yawn on the swampgrass spread-eagled but in collusion? Come, dear audience, to the grape beyond, to the land of wilting glides, let all possessing personalities multiply taut fruition's napeworthy, petulant, suberotic tangle of fabled action—

me, mostly pocket home floods,
                    mostly climb the plagiarism mushroom.

PoÔem 4

A stem then, or a fate, wed
to a wait—clockface insult

strown about the place

A root then, or flowering

rush—perforate synapse

strown about the place

(humble reviewer loses out to talented
editorial fix which is a monkey sound
or wall of sex action heroes meowing)

& O, my heart ith broked.

Poem

The primary catalysts for the decomposition of LSD are heat, light, oxygen, and moisture. LSD's shelf life can be significantly extended if exposure to these are minimized.

Air & Light
Keeping LSD in an air and light proof container is the most important step. A good option is a dark amber glass container kept somewhere cool. Remember, most plastic (plastic bags) is not air tight, though it's a lot better than nothing. Likewise, keeping blotter in foil isn't going to stop air transfer, but it's also better than nothing. If glass isn't available, a combination of foil and plastic would be more effective than either one alone.

Temperature
LSD will degrade even at room temperature, but the hotter the temperature and the longer it is stored in a hot location, the more it will degrade. At room temperature, degradation is quite slow, so a cool room, out of the sun is generally enough to minimize break-down. Storing blotter in the refrigerator or freezer is fine, but is probably unnecessary.

Moisture
If blotter is stored somewhere cold (as opposed to cool), it should be allowed to return to room temperature before being opened as this will prevent condensation from forming. Also, if the weather is extremely humid, storing LSD with a little bit of desiccant (drying agent), can ensure that it stays dry.

If these storage methods are followed, blotter should last for many years. Foil in the freezer is a common storage method, and should be effective at keeping degradation to a minimum for a few years.

Breathing Machine

Day elates the
dissonant daters, & I did too,
deemed waste, the waters
of my spates poorly taint
the grieving leans—

open air, open all, in
governed plots the writhing
gentle staid, unkindly spliced
amidst the yanks the yells portrayed

what amiable mistlike council, debt
to my eyes (the yes) she still, years amidst, a trauma
of beauty torn from the molten web
of games. like all that copied comes
I care again or claim

The Good House, etc.

AN ADDITION

FOR PETER GIZZI

the egretlike alabaster florist
in the red room
is sick—after the healing
he again
is sick—o do not be sick
egretlike alabaster florist
o do not lye ill
o do not rust
egretlike alabaster florist, fellow
helper & wielder of mums,
do not yield to fetid brethren,
the lot of us are tired, also
egretlike,
softening our loons, those of us
that have loons, or know them.

———————

what the closed inside
collapsed, asks, what the laze
lakes, our love of it, home
we have or not, how the kept
apart & the strange
layer the mise-en-scène, merky—

a waning pain, furthering
the excited weights & eyes, a clept
blamelessness, the kissed or etherealed
choosed & painted now—I have made

a let or will
of time or love

———————

o enlisted cleansability
to close me &
achieve or accept the good,
thunder stirs the symbolized
between & is transitory—
a downspouting, circuitous
wild—ailing the limber
stop-motions of the
expansion tank—a town
is more & more disturbed by blame, the latent
emery boards
fingering the window light dry

———————

dearest apparent
dearest well-trained

dearest
        tarantula.
It is a fair question how one
goes about cleaning such a house—
o enlisted cleansability
to close me &
achieve or accept the good,
           a confronted
good,
             the latent emery boards
       fingering the window light dry

—————————

Thunder stirs the symbolized
between & is transitory—
a downspouting, circuitous
wild—
                    the house
has a learning & the house
has a viewfinder—the best
thing in the house though
is an anklet, or a fish poacher
—they have what the skylight
has—which is not what a duct has.

the house in the lake
it is trapped & burdensome,
terrifically inert, sandbagged
& bubbling up—a blatant
casuistry echoes in the
crawlspace—parietal, jipped,
plaster cast, & smarmy—

                    house tells & is told
                    house in the heaving
                    need—woe house
                    woe

                    ———————

it takes great courage
to visit certain homes

                    ———————

the house is made of would
& wonder—forty-five times
no one said it—a
former & future house, with
a dime, & definite—

the house that will save the small
animals from the ravages of inaction
the house that will impel, tiresomely,
a certain gate-kept diplomat's
bureaucratic lechery

the house that refuses the unforetold,
        stymied in the wavering, swanlike,

            —maybe a lakehouse
            w/ a horse
            on a hill,

        hmm.

            ———————

some come to rub on the house & are considered weird

            ———————

pronounced house
but chosen

        house which, tolerant,
        has a bias in its depth

when the painters come
all is quiet, lacking vocabulary,
when the painters come,
bravely through the pine
let them come,
those painters,
let us welcome them,
like so much harm.

    ————————

in the flurry of its
unabetted finality the
unswerving focus on the faulty
good house is the making
of a meaning for the hopefully
unco-opted duration of the heartbeating
habitants & habitat-interactive
humanitarians—

        humbly it hoists
        a kind of void before it,
        housing it, w/ a temper
        of constraint & drama
        talking things over
        waiting to suffice

    ————————

the house is true to pagan
values without withdrawing into
morose antiquarianism—in its
youth, as trees & rubble,
among the plastic plants &
astronomers, the house kept
its council, one might say
it crept into being, displaying
an inner intensity which
was often interpreted as insensitivity—

between the columns & guided
only by the grasped true
character of the almost impossible
columns which guided the only
true character of the almost
impossible columns, between the
columns, to fit the facade, columnar,
w/out impropriety, or commentary
        shadowing what a guest
        might console, columnar,
specifically unjestlike, the
pills coming out of the clock
in the book on the house we
find this true.

———————

The house the house
what of it?

        its frescoes & privvys
      its flagrant livid whiles—

say no to the house

transform its imperiled innards

unbitten, birdlike,
& hot.

—————

The house has mind-read
the noise of conscience
amidst the noise of
modernity, which, like
the sea, seems endless.

  It has become quiet
  in an attempt to escape
  blame. It is a remarkable
  house, here in the help
  & crashing.

—————

Without a tear I can leave this hut
but not w/out a grave—

It has been a good house,
hope it doesn't fall down on you,
hope you keep it up, no house
like it, no siree.

—————

The good house, begun in hope,
hastened toward, has become
the destruction of desire,
which is one of the things we like—

One becomes humble
before the power of the spectacle—
its saturating distrust
& abject extraterritorial
decisiveness send us bills
which we must disguise
from ourselves. These invoices
of terror & what they turn us into—
these heartless apparitions
seeping under the sill—forced
to wear masks & protective garb—
We sit next to our hearts.
Wrankled, waiting it out.

—————

There are not enough particulars
in the house—
not enough soot

Did I mention the house sits
by the railroad tracks. A large
dogwood out in front—
in Virginia, above the public welfare,
below the word & deed, in Virginia,
among the golf balls & swollen books,
late into the evening, wearing Virginia
night, awake, like a house, night-
going, when he is gone.

Poem

rattafrackin frenchies

so just go now

A.G. says hey

Guy says whey, which

hey, today

the "occasional" increases
the occipital (or sompin) &
ain't no flummox-tint high fiving
in the optional nice

which you is so

be well friends

be bon, be good to those other
transparent

teetering

governments

1/98

FOR JENNIFER & STEVE

By the time everything became
what we saw wasn't clear

Altho the prattle
climbs in the collective

combed decision
Breakfast

returns
alongside the lovely landscaped descendant

thoughts of the fire I thought

because the lines
seem to think

of unfrequented
swinging from a fixed point

the medullary cavities, transpicuous,
formed their being into formed

figurative language

so as to transfigure
and part the less shallow, less

transfigurative
crackbrained busts

for determining the dimensionless

knotty, difficult, contracted, confined &
on slight evidence, held

blocks of quartzite
sideboards dis-enveloped, descending

through the advance of its center the sphere
of a reaction which occurs

supporting
a framework

of odd, enveloped
acts or instances

a drunken feastlike limping
impossibly lofty

the intake or exhaust of one who accepts
the northern lights as owner or landlord

the veritable
origin transported by bodies, fluids, or sap

of the heart
to the square
of a spring

resembling this

act of one that casts
a negative vote

of or pertaining to
the pillow of retribution

and the teachings
of ordinary hydrogen

pending some further proceeding affecting
the consequent intermittent upshot

which is usually pretty hard to see, meaning
there are various shades, no pigment,

only pressed ideas, and the light

re-spot

Lastly, the aspects

suspect

the frozen, unfelled

bureaucrats—

their pointy leaky measly quote
thoughts unquote "like"

merriment in an ungoverned macro-titanic
hootin' 'n' tootin'. mine is
the unmunched cointelpro-pop of
cointelpro-pops. the more-fête-than-thou floss-caked

my my my of

nuns on suitcases, eating wafers, of
the sun
in a sailboat, shoop shoop, & Sundays
into Mondays, our little world, shot through

& painted blue,

peaced-out, bleak or pre-bleak, passionately

dangling its neat little plastic misanthropists

out over Davos,

many-colored, forced into a car,

driven to a barn, &

milked.

Summer Poem

The artwork provides the sensuous idea of freedom.

Bed goes up, bed goes down.

Just tie me to me to you.

For clarity's sake.

For a full length feature.

For, or just, orgasmic, like they say.

I have now provided the sensuous idea of freedom.

I'm very pleased you were able to attend.

Moldy Fruition

fizz to inundate the un,
furious points in   flowed
          pre-guttural lips

          & cookies, thin
nether-fascists like rippled leaks is a   chicken lowered

shine back at the symbolic pops of immediate bested fickling

 this &
          the wintering
thought   as if angular
          clarified stuttered seeming, the abrasion named the waking
rents &
               Corrupt governments deceive the christian man.

Camel Light

les guidelines
go
pop
et plus bon
peep
apart
pastie
little
braindead americans
sur la radio
ils parlent
about
good & evil
like
fuff
amidst pills full o'
nuggets &
grandly
conk a punter
's carnegie-sized
belief-system never to
unallow
a smoked astral half-patter
most of 'em

should dispense
a pushed public
joint, break, basted
rateworthy lick-alike or
learn a little
human insensitivity
j'ai envoyé
à
ma tête
tout de suite

Norvo

I am not of muck
rather the made of
EXTRA-MOISTENS
a percentage's neck monk
reimbursement constellation—

errant

the grave, ghost, je me tourne
le monstre technologique
sur l'ange de la *to-come*

like

carrot scraps
in quiet accordions of vanguard transvaluation
the blue penguin speaks
the blue penguin
cuts up his little pink passport with a little pink boxcutter

he thinks you're weird

you think:

the married overcoming of incompetent underbecoming
soothes the bio-mist
a substrata
and superstructed morse-like lemon *amor fati proviso*

pilled like love

pilled with love

Farlow

signed inside a kind of light unreason or maybe syncopating mist tout à fait et
    seeked or blue
same but very quick
the recent or something, we're all yelled
interestin Monday, world's
act in hung and light hung chariot's and
their fat goners, woops I
&
experts are bedded and sassy, half-quilt loonberries
pumped with
a string o' guck, more half-needle than half Carnegie, built
libelous twin bullshit hugging republican cocks
all aligned, all impaired, all exact
as the rasping perilous numbing
currents
lack across their willing bulbs, a
rent ain't a wetness, and a fine figure of $500 or 30
days well that's not facts (cane sugar) that's value (lyric intensity)

Oleo

Don't not dance beside the unburnt sill, whilst burning—
It is not for bricks
this dubious limit
has some raconteurlike fossil collectors & canards people the placebo-sized song of
bathing them.

She's a government employee.

She has lice.

How are you?

manIFpesto

These warnings were not new.

All writing is pigshit.

Amplified recording of a tooth event.

Washington was concerned that Cubans might try to defend themselves.

To have an eye with a brain in it—

drums

it is we who are ominous, the future promises nothing

world's *and*

italic overthrown

expert pentothal peppergum

Again, that makes good sense if hegemony, with its short-term benefits to elite in-
terests, is ranked above survival in the scale of operative values, in accord with the
historical standard for dominant states and other systems of concentrated power.

paste has its reasons, portent
as excess, a plated neat
ruminative—

Love was not
easy

it is about time that we discard all bunkum—

The sphere, ellipses which spin, upside-down cones, spirals and all those dynamic
    forms

taking a bite out of hug cultures

now is not the time for raisins

i need to weep, i guess it's still there

if it tastes like a drain,

cuddle up on the blade and take back your soul—ya know abt this?

maybe we're both wrong

besides i can move this box just fine

the long lost hover

building my own yoga

values absorb Yale law professor Jack Balkin

hissing electric claws absorb Yale law professor Jack Balkin

scenery people, a quote meat background unquote

many believe that surrealism is dead

knowledge systems spreading thru yale law professor Jack Balkin

headwinds, we hate them

new singing sources of heroism, we hate them

how to disrupt meaning in a society in which the head guy says things like "i know how hard it is to put food on yr family"

a praxis of scalp—ya know about this?

author dies, bus pulls away, bus dies too.

look at everything you'll receive when you choose our most popular bundle

this is really man-if-pesto, you can put it on yr spusgetti

Find the job that's right for you.

A Net

(FOR LOVE)

Loud, as is uncommon in this nowhere

The sky, half-fire, half-smoke,

Stops, but continues as a shining wall.

Outside, they who never were,

Loud, unthought nonexistents,

Reaggravated by the nothing.

Stupid one—your wall is all of this.

Raveled

The winded, blind, errant, bi-sected
de-knot
doned—a donate dinning the dry light brace—

same face arrayed, willed
copless, our lovely world, eaten by mice.

Snoopy's Hopeful Pencil

we, on the other hand, watch
little squirrely renumberings, break
them & cost the sun a play

world clubs the tool's new number—he's your neigh-bot
& brokers the coming next

WE'RE ALMOST STOPPED BY SNOOPY'S HOPEFUL PENCIL

4201 Stringfellow Rd Basis Point Badgeless & Blonde

But the pistol was the thing I had so I decided to make a ballot of it and hope for a lucky crowd. Thing One had quieted down and I figured the wax figurine in the Judy Judy had gotten ready to have took a hike accompanied by two pigs, a lamb, and delicate foamy men in white verse forms, their hair like guardians attacking *face* in the final line—they was all up in the joint singing songs about rats and war and chance, la la la, etc. But she had another tactic; suddenly the room was again filled with flotsam. O Great. I peeked out from behind the couch and squinted through. The bag lady was nowhere to be seen. O Great. Only a 3-D projection. So now I knew that the bag lady wasn't behind me. Okay, I thought. Now, where is she? This is not a nub or sundae in the circus feeling. Timbral juxtapositions don't deflate the ego, that's why there's a moon (chokehold) and that's why I like that egg. But it's bad. And it's conscious. Mojave. Pyrrhic intricacies of snuff. Voluntile expertise has a mute button, hopes you'll hold, and wants your info. Full naked area code amassed on the flank & Alleged Sandwich gone gone gone. Loves you. Mwuh. Hugga hugga. Spornapple swish-lick whenever will you come (free love free verse free diskettes . . . But the egg in the bag lady's gun lucked out. We won. Twice. Nothing ever happens here. In this cursed one horse town. Nothin but some drinkin an shoutin. Little flotsam. Little flecks of scraped innards threadbare glory lookalikes and their mammals. Maybe a moat, cain't really tell. And my goat hurts. Lackey-wanna-cracker etc. Relieve Me You. First, fires, second, the wrecking of threshing, third, the parish poor handpicked straight from the dock, fourth, salmon, fifth, salmon, sixth, salmon. Fuckin salmon all over the place. Fuckin healthy social salmon identities and their spaceship helpers. Whaddya gonna do? Salmon, that's what. Labourers seldom live under their employers' roofs for these very reasons.

L'identité est la cause des verrues

j'ai un crapaud. il s'appelle buber. buber le crapeau. buber élève des lapins. les lapins vivent dans une grande poubelle qui s'appelle grande poubelle. ou poubelle à lapins. la plupart du temps ils se plaignent. buber tape sur le couvercle pour qu'ils se calment. ça ne marche pas. à la dernière réunion annuelle du fonds monétaire international, buber a parlé de trucs de crapauds devant une salle comble. il a bien baratiné & les banquiers ont tapé sur leurs couvercles. parfois buber et moi fumons un joint. d'autres fois pendant qu'il est en train de taper il a un petit spasme de sympathie mais toujours pour lui-même & il appelle au téléphone & le téléphone dit n'importe quoi alors il tape aussi dessus & j'ai de la peine pour le téléphone & moi je reste en plan avec toutes ces autres choses dans la pièce à me poser des questions au sujet de ce crapaud tapeur dans ma vie. buber prend un air de Eh ben ça alors! qui chez les crapauds ressemble à toutes leurs autres expressions mais ce crapaud-là chante « Ma p'tite je bosse pas dans une usine à bonbons/ Nan & je vends pas de chewing-gum » eh les mecs si vous avez des crapauds. pouvez-vous m'aider à sortir de mes problèmes de crapauds. des fois je passe des nuits blanches à dormir. j'en ai marre partout. des fois je pense que je devrais plutôt prendre une grenouille mais mon pote jigs casey a une grenouille & il a fabriqué une arme nucléaire avec & je serais extrêmement reconnaissant que vous ne m'appeliez plus.

[screened in]

bluffed
churning's caught
learning's bent
leaving plates
sexual heretofore's
coarsening
flux—the runned
& powdered
circulate
late
in the world's
writing's enigmatic
tactic-faced care-thief
an importance bite
brace
of things
buried
(bluffed & lucrative)
(bluffed & inner) bluffed
& crazed

~~Pygal Shield~~

afterfeathering obverse
insectivorous pusher—

We're crepidona—

wholemeal halfwits in the bunker silo's
frontal sinus palate polojama
or else
jumpsuit, yet
the sighting mirror
centerspan
clogs the thongs & pumps welding
the refueling probe's washing
counterweight to the cliff's
pushbutton balaclava

fall up, orange in the grapeleaf, upper in the
upper lateral lobe

The Lyric Republican

the reasons flake off
of a died news roundup
exculpating dim fish—join us
in our mountain flowers, meet us
as rats
imitating
the horizon

maybe their worshipping their oaths
has a kind of shaking hook bed index we can flame

meet Riyadh, meet the present participle of "to go"

war herbs,

be proved,

I hate

had been jerks are little storelike haunted lycopenes
dipped in our kernel of a nothing

better to sit aside feeding truth to a pig

Elitist Crap Bag

This elitist crap does not one any good.
I'm damn tired of reading posts by musical elitist punks who think.
I've never understood this elitist crap
It's very confusing trying to figure out what an elitist is these days
crap about elitism flourishes.
elitist crap. It's too bad
but this 'elitist' crap
promotes the exact elitist crap you espouse
Both of which are piles of elitist crap.
Cmon.
I hope you realize I'm not going to subsidize this elitist crap
with my tax dollars! Update:
We don't need none of that fancy-pants elitist education crap. Update:
Woeful has added Useless Crap For Your Enjoyment (Education)
Funny thing is, us "elitists" want to help the rest of you get better
education, better jobs
Typical elitist crap. No, I agree.
Picasso said that same thing
The elitist love to make fun of us common crap
My problem is the crap
Thanks, from your favorite elitist crap bag
You are an arrogant, classist, elitist, file wienie. Your line of crap
Sells because fools like you are allowed to continue regurgitating
but the real Elitists are made in Hasbro, with real crap . . .

"Squeeze the Eagle Club!"

Fairy's inhabit
How do you say, um,
Flakey people—& are restless,
need angst to spill
on vagrance—the red shadows, softly
up, equal
How do you say, um,
these befated fat future metaphysicians
requesting the floor, workin' the door
& yet *we're* competent, pesky in the face
of those who overvalue attitude, direct speech,
patience, &/or flotsam. Stop valuing
the surprise, stop not too often, stop
&   this is another poem called

Ordinance Disposal Satellite

the downed
letting stares the rote, slyly uncopes, steeps. A western
oversaying layed soft across the modillion, the playbill
sent—lathed platypus awning
& culpable once
which harbors.

Me's Wittl Birdy Bong Stowy

I boughted my wittl pairwukete
a birdy bong for hims birfday

but it gived him a itty wittle cut on hims
bitty wittle beak-wip couldn't do a bawwel woll

i don't know y-cuz
i mean it was hims wip not

hims wittle wingys so i sd
to hims wittle birdy-wirdy

which was not hims namey-wamey
the dawk suwwounds us nummy-wummy googly woo

Hoo's got a wittle bitty potty mouth?
Why you!

win

the world which taut
the wink how to smash—
tri-grid winds successfully
smell causation, perk in
branching on the soft blamed
clammy. a waif
studiously mooches or else
strums. bodily
triumvirate like a broken
book's pulsing on the
day.

Buoyancy

The light then. The singing in the letters
which are gnats which if windy . . .

See then, the fool who comes to you
& forgets to bring his joy. Who thinks
he will find it with you.

Everything I have written is trash. I have not
even the strength to love. Let it go.
That's true that is not true. Untrained
tandem gnat-brain if you want the city
and dying fish to be a touchstone rub
the indicator needle & a genie will
appear, knitting. I'm sorry for saying
I loved you when I've not really done
that. But o I have in my foolish batter
head, in my back, too tight, the frog
voice underneath.

Everything, trash & strength. Let it go.
All of them. I am lead when I should be
salt, or else gum when I should be
gunk. Go back go back to the drinking
place souls that snow. The quivering

obliged no more at rest & joy. Soft
is a world should perish. & the victory
of the light.

I Ching say "He ends by achieving nothing."
A real devotee, no? Invited from
blank & obtained, another bed
for interrupting, perhaps the
world's. You said you were
the world. Well, maybe. Because
a calf thinks god is a cow.

I have to write past this obsession
with you, Nora, with an invalid
admiration in the learning. You've
got the idea. I'm a calf. & the victory
of the light.

Does it go on? The poem I mean.
Between tortoise & torture you'll
find and analyze a repetition fetish
& accidental death pretending
we're supposed to recover that's
what the pills are for. That's not what
the pills are for. The victory of the
light tho, is gentle, I believe that.

        The love has almost
destroyed me. So he begged.
A calf, yes. And a source of

light, & a digestive tract. Sense
& the great friend. Found & alone.
I am your mirror, here are the stones.
That was stolen, & no longer is. That's
true that is not true, & trash.

Some things forgive. People always
do, whether they die or not. Eventually.
Somehow. Opening. Your heart's
bad. Half of it. How come? My heart's
horrendous. A thief-book. Held wrong
at twelve, half-loved. Poetry is
truly remarkable trash.

Poem

It must be tough to be a bug in the rain.

Infinity Revisited

As I said to my Spontaneously Obese Rat Friend, I said

The aim of this poem is to assess weather produced from rat feed, grain,
and four doses. The study used 480 male and female rats
and their little rat cell phones (under Simulated Microgravity)
which did not have cancer. One will study acupuncture.
The other will look at the old rats. Words from the Simon
and Garfunkle song, that ol' one, incorporated into rat their rat anterior pituitary
     Like a rat in a maze, the path before me &
One rat out of 23 failed to develop &
      Hooked heads of little rodent swimmers &
For the student of behavioral study; or; a pet rat keeper
this book is tops!~
Cell Phones Don't Cause Cancer, Rat Finds God, OBVIOUSLY
THAT RAT
should not perform mechanistic multigenerational neuroscientists
anymore. In one of these studies, Yamagata et al.
The mean live weight. Cultured at 5%.
RAT TUMOR CELLS! RAT TUMOR CELLS! which clearly means:
Ben comma (acapella) uncomma
Hints that one drink a day during pregnancy may be dangerous.
the apoptosis OF EITHER
tail or ears
. in rats . the IC rat 4-day oral toxicity

and approximate lethal doses

at checkout.

Voltage-sensing Domain and Peptide Gating

exhibited its first typical "neurotic pattern" outside

one of the funnier case studies i have i mean

they're fucking rats for crying out loud. give a rat a chance

they're fucking rats

These include the finding of nasal proliferative lesions in a rat

of KFC

IN. RAT. TISSUES .... one epi. the other the

the finding of nasal

branches

from the PUBLIC LIBRARY OF SCIENCE. period.

Study of a Breast. period. the

Cancer Rat Model with Compound the

Reports of well-performed scientific studies from all

times indicated

Can Supplements Improve Aging?

(The rats were randomly assigned to consume one of four experimental diets)

from all times

indicated (in spite of the tennis)

Release from Rat Mast! (rat study finds

and the Mouse . . .

Lipid in Zucker

and the Mouse . . .

Lipid in Zucker

Tables 1–6 show the results obtained

vivo accumulation in a rat prostate

air at

corticoste. . . . behavior

phosphatidylethanolamine binding

one rat died and another was euthanized

One limitation of the study, the researchers said,

one rat died and another was euthanized, the researchers said,

Four succumbed to pressure, and only one survived.

Black Marble

                                        in the age
                                        of art as
                                        whatever the submodernists
                                        are masking the
                                        classicist countdown's sachet-
                                        sickness so as
                                        to undercomfort miffed
                                        barflylike aptitude—

                    —the rasping
            courtly muffins—

                    —the nare-do-well excess
            accompaniment

                            uncompelled & disclosed, loaning
                            nobody
                            soup but
                                    some of them leave
                                    & have many other
                                            important things
                                            to do.

A Fire

Free in the excessive
re-knit
business of rinse, a raid lather open
a not-so
you-then fairly twisted pencil shaver

weedle weedle

The moneys that these arms sales bring in
are just one part of a wonderful, simple,
yet cohesive strategy to improve our lives—
you see, by contributing to global disorder
and fear, by maiming the possibility
of meaningful education, and destroying
large numbers of mammals we contribute
to the possible continued hegemony
of our little nationalist construct thus
ensuring continued availability in this
area of important products like raspberry
toothpaste and red or green pepper
spray.

I'm a little mailbox, short and stout
here is my clear mind and broken spine
here is my intellect bla bla bla

beed

so I was walking
in the park
today
and I saw
this bee
and I accidentally
flung my body
on top of it
so all these
bees came flying
forth and I got
beed

This is such total bullshit.

at the political
consciousness exhibition
a blameless
weasel
infected by petty
blown about
weasel ideoglossia
or some upper-echelon
America loves you
Billy Bob Thorntonodious, tiresome, obnoxious
critiquing of your review of
bullshit propaganda
well, Fuck you, Bartender
Wait, how the fuck old are you?
How do you sleep at night? What?
Fuck the Carter Administration
Robots wash my car for me
doofus   What? YES THEY DO
I don't make this shit up
The reason I bring this up is
Shut the fuck up
Here's to experiences revolving around food bringing you up
you fucking choke

And man, if you haven't seen muppets fucking
you really need to get out more

Time

or its tons o' swordlike trills
taupe in the croode, thin
nether-fops loose like raining
Pleiades—peace hath a recombinant
bather's embraced pillage—
in the repentant empire
in the unguzzled longtemps
in the resonant tri-fed tout
—plasticized & patient
mores clang in the capable
folk—they are war &
win the time like lice like
shown a board they would
signal the
Beads of concepts, choke
the suns a part

Story

Blooded, loopy, ingenious, & pasty

The ferile haberdasher dopes his trunk-master

& drives off to Vegas where kiwi-God, a kind of donette,

Drips all over his Ashbery-sized Bay

window.

Nordic Cudgelhead

cud-monk in the given

row-row-row like a morphine-sized
rigamarole—the vest fits the missing

deathwatch, has all the trimmings, & slow boss-incised
bitter yet limber

beat-me-ups barricade the bot in the scissor—

that's the feel good movie

that's the barely stained low-fat brain

**There is nothing that
is not appropriation.**

what they said or didn't
doesn't
to give you an
idea
talk more about
deep
pressure forming
all around my eyes

or rather,

what they said or didn't
doesn't
to give you an
idea
talk more about
deep
pressure forming
all around my eyes

      "   "

songed or,

act—the resting
subtle lunch:
sold-out, like a planar
obsolescent rendering's
nut-blubbered threading

then, coyly,
sorrow's drypoint
bepetment, lucky there,
calls me back, cloaked in
candled song, just a real
amorphous dust

intonation, the jailer's
art a purple exception, leap
then a cent—we people that
all over oil, & drain
the re-sent, clarion, bastardizations

Three Cigarette Poems

Not an organ exactly
but it has a theme—

futility as figurative
extreme:

    them electro-tones
    erase
    feathered statuary

   please papa put it on the
patisserie—

   the plate

   maven in the recent
   reindustrialized pre-pack

   makes me wash up &

   it's cryin'

6/30 9:05 PM
CAMEL LIGHT

it's an inaugural diagonNal
incomprehension called

help me with my homework

listen
I don't like it either.
ack.

ripe like a
Roman poem
      Pleasure is the last half
      of the matter
      (it disappears)
Put that in yr life &
you're late for work

History Ends in Green

      hope so.

6/21   3:55 PM

AMERICAN SPIRIT

we disabuse
it bounteously
—this breakage—

I'm not a-coordinated husk

No actual o'clock to back-
order being

in it, but then, viable
prices wouldn't prizefight
night's moralia's mega-fun

the coupling ordinary

that nary a tag end

loosens

5/23   12:51 AM

HARLEY-DAVIDSON LIGHT

10:49 PM

light of surface & light
of morrows, we told it like we should, lit
clock in the hot blue-cotton hoot, nearly
yielding, on the table's plastic
tone, &, being creation, a total
crosswise outsider, loved, the five euphoric
towns' natural pretext etiquette the dancing
conscious moon

Dimmer's Data for Your Dad's Dumb Idea about a Dumpster

Yeah yeah, it's true, minimalism a kind of curds & weigh, but o how it rocketh Cassandra's little bourgeois-flavored mnemonotechnicisms. I know that's not sayin a lot, it's lucky that way . . . It is in this then that the cursory aspecticized semiconsciousness of spectacular special plait e-diners leaven the meritorious heartfelt mythologizing we need so bad. The rolling hills. The unraised garments. The reading courses. Hurrah. If he weren't a climber, he'd jump. There's no encoded logic to the mourning peasant's colicky expectorizing. & neither should there be. The artwork provides the sensuous idea of freedom.

Go With Your Gut

Loops of the small bowel
fight spam on the internet.
The search is over.
Should You Really be Concerned?
empanadas, glorious lobster creations,
and chicken bagel nerves.
I've got chicken bagel nerves.
"Hey, I no come work today, I sick,
headache, stomach ache, leg,
free speech."

Personally, I go to bed early
after watering the Catwort.
It's just what I do.

Sometimes when I have stomachache,
I lie face down in some internet.

Poem (A Chance of Rain)

FOR HEATHER FULLER

o figuera, o my stumps
mossing up the rocket lane
o figuera, o my stumps
drams in pastures cap
or collapse

                that
          uncoordinated
          sunshiney liming

            it's a glum triad—

              it tears me up

    o figuera, o my stumps

        Doors still start with a d
        on days that leave abrupt—
        dried up

o figuera, o my stumps

losing unconcerned salt

on the retread latent   death of sleep

o figuera, o my stumps

the distortion task attic

to unhinge mastication error

in the wax it atrophies

the mazy prow is mute

o figuera, o my stumps

(I have a mental sore throat)

(they're putting fragments in the coup)

Treatise on Consequences

just intonation   See temperament
impurities of stellar evolution

a guide surrounding the blocks

metal curvatures

Thus, if the body

A device
photographed with the water
which is fixed
to a diaphragm in contact
with the water

The focal length
because the eye lens
envelope these wavelets

exchange force
a reversible change
mounted on a process

mains-powered
dissociation decay, of love
in the iron oxide paste

either spontaneously
or following a collision

edge dislocation   see defect

solved food
(the speed of reliability)
or
the process of boiling
light committing bodies

see a substance that can
sustain positioned stops

hole condition   *see* hole
but in words

The problem of pain

a thermocouple in most cases
cyclically maudlin
&/or
magnetically extreme

savoir salve

floor to fix missed

(very early)
very between the terminals

"hence the excited state
is relatively long-lived"

internal ampere
exit, form defined as
soapy mounting

perhaps a short pump
with a shaking frequency band

Crosstalk—
the biblical faith
when we add a pinch
becomes mathematic

How do you plead?

the commonest is to heat
as just wandering is to hands

Some of these poems have appeared in the following publications: *Abraham Lincoln, Apartment Poetry, Barque, Beltway Quarterly, Bon Voyage!, The Brooklyn Rail, Critical Quarterly, Eleven Eleven, The Hat*, the *i.e.* broadside series, *PhillyTalks, Siblia, West Wind Review*, and the *Woodland Pattern* broadside series, as well as the chapbook *You Bête* (Abraham Lincoln, 2011). The poem "*L'identité est la cause des verrues*" ("Identity Is the Cause of Warts") appears in the chapbook *Poèmes de l'araignée* (Un bureau sur l'Atlantique, 2002), which was the result of a translation seminar conducted at the Fondation Royaumont in 2002. The collective translation was led by Emmanuel Hocquard and included the translators Etel Adnan, Pascale Casanova, Patricia Chen, Lionel Cuillé, Joseph Guglielmi, Françoise de Laroque, and Pascale Petit. "Poem" beginning "the primary catalysts" was taken from a website that has now disappeared though the text can still be found on message boards at bluelight, erowid, Yahoo, and elsewhere on the web. "Find the job that's right for you." was taken from the Andy Warhol Museum website circa 2008. The author would like to thank the authors, editors, publishers, and translators of these publications. Thanks also to everyone in the DC Poetry crowd whose daily support makes the work possible, and to my editor Joshua Beckman and friend Peter Gizzi for their active attention to the manuscript of this book.